YOU CHOOSE
BOOKS

D0284104

THE QUEST OF
THESEUS

AN INTERACTIVE MYTHOLOGICAL ADVENTURE

by Blake Hoena
illustrated by Carolyn Arcabascio

Consultant: Dr. Laurel Bowman
Department of Greek and Roman Studies
University of Victoria
Victoria, British Columbia, Canada

CAPSTONE PRESS
a capstone imprint

You Choose Books are published by Capstone Press,
1710 Roe Crest Drive, North Mankato, Minnesota 56003
www.mycapstone.com

Library of Congress Cataloging-in-Publication Data
Names: Hoena, B. A., author.
Title: The quest of Theseus : an interactive mytholoical adventure /
by Blake Hoena.
Other titles: You choose books. You choose Greek myths.
Description: North Mankato, Minnesota : Capstone Press, 2017. |
Series: You choose books. Ancient Greek myths
Identifiers: LCCN 2016032389 (print) |
LCCN 2016033187 (ebook)
ISBN 9781515748212 (library binding)
ISBN 9781515748267 (pbk.) | ISBN 9781515748304 (eBook PDF)
Subjects: LCSH: Theseus, King of Athens—Juvenile literature. |
Plot-your-own stories.
Classification: LCC BL820.T5 H635 2017 (print) |
LCC BL820.T5 (ebook) | DDC 398.20938/02—dc23
LC record available at https://lccn.loc.gov/2016032389

Editorial Credits
Mandy Robbins, editor; Ted Williams, designer;
Kelly Garvin, Media researcher; Katy LaVigne, production specialist

Illustrations by Carolyn Arcabascio; cover illustration by Nadine Takvorian

Image Credits
Shutterstock/Timur Kulgarin, 98

Artistic elements: Shutterstock: Alex Novikov, Eky Studio, reyhan, Samira
Dragonfly, Tymonko Galyna,

Printed and bound in Canada.
010050S17

Table of Contents

About Your Adventure

YOU are the mighty Greek hero Theseus. You are on a quest to find your long-lost father, King Aegeus, and make him proud. Your ultimate goal is to become the heir to the king's throne. Your quest has you facing monsters, criminals, and powerful gods. You must defeat them all if you are to prove your worth to your father.

Chapter One sets the scene. Then you choose which path to take. Follow the directions at the bottom of each page. The choices you make determine what happens next. After you finish your path, go back and read the others for more adventures.

YOU CHOOSE the path you take through this mythical adventure.

A Father's Sword

"Theseus, I have a surprise for you," your mother says. "Come."

You grab your cloak and follow her outside. She leads you through the streets of Troezen, your home city. You pass shops and thatched homes. All the while, your mother is silent.

"Where are we going?" you ask.

"Just follow me," your mother whispers.

She leads you out of town. Eventually the marketplace and houses are left behind. Once Troezen is no longer in sight, your mother turns onto a narrow path that winds its way up a hill.

Turn the page.

"You're old enough now," she begins. "It's time I told you the truth about your father."

This comes as a surprise. Your father left Troezen before you were born. Until now, your mother wouldn't tell you who he was. She'd never told anyone the truth.

When people asked, your mother said that you were the son of Poseidon. Living near the sea, the people of Troezen honored him above all other gods. He was the city's patron. So when your mother, Princess Aethra, claimed that Poseidon was your father, no one argued. They did not want to risk angering the mighty sea god. But you never really believed her.

"You've probably guessed that Poseidon is not your father," your mother whispers.

"Does anyone else know that?" you ask.

"Only your grandfather," she says. "He's the only one who knows the truth."

"But why did you lie to everyone, including me, all these years?" you wonder aloud.

In the past, you had begged your mother to tell you who your father really was. She always stuck to her claim that it was Poseidon.

She stops and turns to you. "I'm sorry," she says. "I wanted to, but your father—your real father—had warned me not to."

"Why?" you ask. "Why keep it a secret?"

"To protect us, to keep you safe," your mother says. "Your father has many enemies."

She turns away and starts walking the rest of the way up the hill.

"Then who is he?" you ask, chasing after her.

Turn the page.

"King Aegeus of Athens," your mother says.

You are stunned. You had guessed your father might be an important man. But never had you imagined he would rule one of the most important cities in all of Greece.

"Your father was on his way home from seeing the Oracle of Delphi," your mother explains. "He wanted an heir, and the oracle's guidance led him to me. But before you were born, King Minos of Crete declared war on Athens. Your father left to defend his city."

"Why didn't he come back to see you?" you ask. "To see me?"

Your mother bows her head. "He couldn't."

Athens had lost the war with Crete, and there are rumors of a horrible price the city has been forced to pay. You don't know the full story. Maybe that is what kept your father away all these years.

"But he left some gifts for you," your mother says. "In case he could not return."

"What are they? Where are they?" you ask.

"There," your mother says, pointing to a large rock. It is about as big around as you are tall.

"I don't understand," you say, confused.

"Your father said that once you were grown I was to bring you here," your mother explains. "He wanted me to tell you about the gifts. He said they are yours if you can move that rock."

You have nothing of your father's. If he left something for you, you want it.

Determined, you strut over to the rock. You plant your feet and push with all your strength. Your legs tremble. Ever so slightly, you feel the rock shift.

Turn the page.

Bit by bit, the rock moves. With one last burst of strength, you roll it aside.

"You did it!" your mother says, proudly.

Where the rock once sat is a hole. In it, you find a sword and a pair of sandals.

You reach down to pull out the sandals. You swap your footwear for your father's. Then you take the sword and hold it up to examine.

"With this blade, I will make my father proud," you promise.

Now, you are ready to prove yourself as one of Greece's greatest heroes. But what adventure will you go on?

To become the rightful heir to the throne of Athens, turn to page 15.

To battle the Minotaur, turn to page 49.

To venture into the Underworld, turn to page 75

Chapter 2

The Journey to Athens

As you hold your father's sword, you tell your mother, "I will go see my father. I will earn the right to be heir to the throne of Athens."

As you prepare to leave, your mother tells you some alarming news.

"I've heard your father is about to be married to Medea," she says.

"The witch who helped Jason and the Argonauts retrieve the Golden Fleece?" you ask. Everyone in Greece has heard of how Jason earned the right to rule Iolcos by finding this priceless treasure.

Turn the page.

Your mother nods. "Medea has a son, Medus. If you don't reach your father before the wedding, Medus will become heir to your father's throne."

Now you have another reason to hurry. You gather up your things and prepare to leave.

"Be careful," your mother warns.

"I will," you reply as you hug her.

You take the road out of Troezen that heads north. It will take you past the city of Epidaurus and to the Isthmus of Corinth. From there, you will go east, around the gulf's northern shore, and on to Athens.

The farther you get from home, the fewer travelers you see. The ones you do come across clutch their belongings close. This worries you. Why are people so nervous?

"Excuse me," you say to an elderly man. "What dangers lie along this road?"

The man appears to be afraid of you.

"I mean you no harm," you say. "I'm on my way to Athens."

"I wouldn't take the road to Epidaurus, then," the man says. "There are thieves, and Periphetes is the worst of them."

"I've never heard of him," you say.

"He's a giant, about twice as tall as I am," the man explains. "They call him Clubman because of the weapon he carries."

You could continue along the road you are on. But traveling by water might be safer, and it would also be quicker.

To stay on the road, turn to page 18.

To travel by boat, turn to page 19.

You feel sorry for the old man and offer him some food. Then you continue on to Athens.

Even though danger lies ahead, you stay on the road to Epidaurus. After all, you are out to prove yourself. What better way than by facing a giant?

For a few hours, you see no other travelers. Then, as you round a bend, your path is blocked. The giant Periphetes stands before you. He rests a large iron club on one shoulder.

"Hand over your valuables if you know what's good for you," the giant grunts.

Then he takes a clumsy step toward you. While the upper half of his body is incredibly muscular, he has thin, weak legs and walks with a bad limp.

To fight the giant with your father's sword,
turn to page 21.

To wrestle the giant's club away from him, turn to page 22.

You thank the old man and say goodbye. You worry about what lies ahead. You want to reach your father as quickly as you can. You don't want to risk facing a giant before seeing him.

At the next town, a fisherman offers you a ride in his boat to Kineta, a small town on the northern shore of the Saronic Gulf. This way you can avoid the giant.

Once Kineta is in sight, the fisherman says, "I can't risk taking you any farther. A giant sea turtle lurks under the cliff up ahead. I've heard it will snatch up anyone who gets close to its lair."

The fisherman sets you ashore. You thank him for getting you this far. You are again walking along the road to Athens. Only now, you are more than halfway to your destination.

Turn the page.

As you head east, the road winds its way up the rocky cliff that overlooks the Saronic Gulf. Near the top, a man stops you. He grips a spear as he shouts down to you.

"Greetings, traveler," he says. "My name is Sciron, and none may pass this way without doing me a favor first."

"What might that be?" you ask, curious.

Sciron lifts up one foot. He does not wear any shoes, and his foot is encrusted with dirt.

"Wash my feet," he says with a smile.

To do as Sciron asks, turn to page 25.

To refuse Sciron's request, turn to page 26.

Your father left you his sword for a reason—to use! You draw your weapon.

"So that's how it will be," Periphetes snarls.

He hefts his club over his head and brings it crashing down. You leap back as it slams into the ground with a THWUMP!

Periphetes has muscular arms, and his club is longer than your sword. You can't get close to him. Every time you try to attack, you have to duck or leap aside as the giant's club whirs through the air.

You dash around him, hoping to attack from behind, but the giant whips his club around. Before you can react, Periphetes delivers a crushing blow, ending your life.

THE END

To follow another path, turn to page 12.

To learn more about Theseus, turn to page 99.

"Your valuables, now!" Periphetes shouts.
"Or you'll find out why they call me the Clubman."

You had already guessed it is because of the
huge club that he shakes at you with his thick,
strong arms. But you have also noticed the giant's
weakness. You grab the club as he jabs it at you
and tug with all your might. The giant is pulled
off balance and tips forward on his thin, weak legs.
To keep from falling, he has to let go of the club.
Now the mighty weapon is yours!

"Your thieving ways are done!" you shout.

With one blow, you strike down the giant.

You are surprised at how easy it is to wield the
club. You decide to keep the weapon as your own.
You continue on to Corinth, knowing that the road
will now be much safer for travelers.

Turn the page.

As you walk, you hear someone cry, "Help!"

You crest a hill and see a large man struggling with a pine tree. He has a rope tied to its top and is trying to bend its tip to the ground.

"My name is Sinis," the man shouts to you. "Could you give me a hand?"

"What are you doing?" you ask, confused.

"I'll tell you when I'm finished," he grunts. "Just help me pull this treetop to the ground."

You decide it can't hurt to help. Together you bend the tree down to the ground.

"I need to stake it down," Sinis says, "Just hold tight for a second."

This seems odd. You're unsure what to do.

To hold onto the tree, turn to page 29.

To let go of the tree, turn to page 30.

Sciron has the high ground. You doubt you could defeat him in battle. His feet are filthy. But you need to get to Athens, so you agree.

"Sit there," he says, pointing to a bench near the edge of the cliff.

You sit facing Sciron. Your back is to the gulf.

"The water bucket is behind you," he says.

You turn to grab it. Suddenly, Sciron kicks you, catching you off guard. You tumble over the cliff and splash into the water below.

As you thrash about, a giant shape rises from the depths. It is the sea turtle the fisherman warned you about. It snatches you up in its powerful jaws. You drown as it drags you down to its lair.

THE END

To follow another path, turn to page 12.

To learn more about Theseus, turn to page 99.

"No," you say. "I'm in a hurry."

Sciron smiles. "Then you have no choice."

Sciron has the high ground. It would be easier for him to strike you with his spear than for you to use your sword. But you can outsmart him.

"Okay," you say. "Show me what I need to do."

"Just sit there," he says, pointing to a bench at the edge of the cliff.

You walk to the bench and remember the giant sea turtle. You guess what Sciron has planned. You spin around just as he is about to shove you and knock him aside. Sciron loses his balance. He splashes into the sea below. The giant sea turtle quickly snatches him up. Sciron just suffered the fate he had planned for you. Relieved, you continue on your way to Athens.

Turn the page.

Before you reach Athens, you travel through Eleusis. As you approach the city, a large man steps onto the road and blocks your path.

"You're a strong young man," he says. "Why don't you test your strength against me?"

You want to prove yourself, but you didn't expect so many challenges on the way to Athens. You must get there before your father's wedding.

"I'm in a hurry," you say.

But as you try to walk past, he stops you.

"I am Cercyon, ruler of Eleusis," he explains. "If you can out-wrestle me, I will reward you with riches from my kingdom."

Cercyon steps back to await your answer.

To accept Cercyon's challenge, turn to page 33.

To quickly continue on to Athens, turn to page 34.

"OK, I've got it," you say to Sinis.

You grip the tree, pulling with all your weight.

"Are you holding on tight?" Sinis asks.

"Yes!" you shout, through gritted teeth.

Then suddenly Sinis lets go. Your weight alone isn't enough to keep the tree bent down. And you are so determined to hold on that you don't let go. The tree snaps upright. By the time you realize what's happening, it's too late. You are flung high into the sky.

"Ahhhhhh!" you scream, sailing through the air.

Eventually gravity brings you crashing down. You die instantly as you smack into the ground.

THE END

To follow another path, turn to page 12.

To learn more about Theseus, turn to page 99.

"Are you holding on tight?" Sinis asks slyly.

There is something about him that makes you nervous. You don't quite trust him.

"Why are we doing this?" you ask again.

"Just hold on while I get a rope from my pocket."

With one hand, he helps you hold onto the tree. With the other, he reaches into his pocket.

Suddenly, Sinis tries to wrap the rope around your wrists. You leap back to escape and let go of the tree. Sinis is caught leaning over the tree, and his weight alone can't hold it down. The tree snaps upright. Sinis is flung high into the sky. He screams as he sails through the air.

Sinis comes crashing back down and lands with a THWUMP. You realize Sinis has just suffered the death he had planned for you.

Turn the page.

You continue on your journey. As you near the town of Crommyon, you hear rumors of a terrible wild pig called the Crommyonian Sow. The beast has stampeded through farms, smashing stables and digging up fields.

When you reach Crommyon, everyone is hiding in their homes. You see the beast's tracks in the dirt streets. Its hoofprints are as large as your hands.

"It must be gigantic," you whisper to yourself.

A man rushing down the street overhears you. "She is an awful beast!" the man cries as he runs.

These people are in danger, and you might be able to help them. Do you have time to hunt down the Crommyonian Sow yourself? Or should you hurry on to Athens and get help from your father?

To continue on to Athens, turn to page 36.

To hunt down the Crommyonian Sow, turn to page 38.

"If I win, I can have all the riches in your kingdom?" you ask, to be sure you heard correctly.

He smiles and nods. Defeating Cercyon would earn you fame. And showing up in Athens rich would be even better.

You accept the challenge, and Cercyon charges. You grapple with him, but he is stronger than you.

"By the way," he says, "this fight is to the death."

He reaches out to crush you with his muscular arms. But you slip from his grasp. You must use Cercyon's strength against him. He charges, and you duck. He falls across your shoulders, and you slam him down to the ground. He lies at your feet, dead.

But the people of Eleusis are angry that you have killed their king. They give you no riches. You continue on to Athens feeling disappointed.

Turn to page 39.

"I have no time for this nonsense," you tell Cercyon. "I need to see my father, King Aegeus of Athens," you reply.

Cercyon is impressed and steps out of your way.

"Very well then," he says. "If that is indeed true, be on your way, young prince."

You smile as you brush past Cercyon. No one has ever called you a "prince" before. You will be glad to see your father and make that title official. You continue to follow the coast as it curves southward, toward Athens.

The city is in sight when four riders approach. Two soldiers escort a woman and her child. They stop in front of you.

"Greetings," the woman says. "My friend Cercyon sent me a message that King Aegeus's son was on his way to Athens."

"I am he," you say. "Who are you?"

"Medea," she says. Motioning to the boy, she adds, "And this is my son, Medus, soon to be the rightful heir to Athens."

"But I'm the king's eldest son," you argue.

"Not any more," Medea says.

The soldiers draw their swords. You hold your club, ready for them. But suddenly you can't move. An eerie voice sings, "Be still, be still, against your will." Medea has cast a spell on you!

Unable to defend yourself, the soldiers easily strike you down. You breathe your last breath.

THE END

To follow another path, turn to page 12.

To learn more about Theseus, turn to page 99.

You decide to hurry to Athens. You will persuade your father to send help to Crommyon.

Once in Athens, you tell a pair of city guards that you have news of the Crommyonian Sow to tell the king. They take you to your father in the palace. At his side sits Medea.

"Father," you cry, showing him the sword.

The king's eyes light up. But then Medea whispers to him, and his expression goes dark.

"Did you kill this beast, the Crommyonian Sow?" he asks.

"No," you admit. "I came here to seek help."

"No son of Aegeus would let that monster continue to threaten his people," Medea cries.

"How did you get that sword?" the king asks.

"From the spot where you hid it," you say.

Again, Medea whispers to the king. Whatever she said is filling your father with doubt.

"How could a son of mine let a beast go on threatening people?" he scolds.

"Guards!" Medea shouts.

"Father!" you plead, as guards take you away.

You are dragged from the throne room and tossed into the palace's dungeon. You hope that King Aegeus will give you another chance to prove yourself. But that night, after eating the slop the jailor served, you feel a wrenching pain in your belly. As you gasp for breath, you realize you have been poisoned. Medea's evil smile is the last thing you remember.

THE END

To follow another path, turn to page 12.

To learn more about Theseus, turn to page 99.

You can't leave the people of Crommyon. They need protection. Perhaps defeating the sow will prove your worth as a leader to your father.

You follow the tracks in the mud. They lead to a hilly, forested area. Along the way, you see knocked-over trees. You are on the right path.

You climb the next hill and spot the beast wallowing in a pond. It snorts as it picks up your scent. Then the sow leaps out of the water. It is nearly as tall as you, with foot-long tusks.

You raise Periphetes's club as the wild pig charges. Just as the sow is within reach, you slam the club down on its head with bone-crunching force.

The people of Crommyon will be safe from this beast from now on. Now you must continue on your journey to Athens.

Your mother was right. The road to Athens is filled with danger. You hope that tales of your quest will reach your father and make him proud.

You still have a little way to go to reach Athens. It is getting dark. Up ahead, you hear the hammering from a blacksmith's shop. Perhaps you could sleep there tonight. A man greets you.

"I am Procrustes," he says. "You look weary. Do you need a place to spend the night?"

You sit down and have dinner with Procrustes. Then he shows you to his only bed.

"You can sleep here for the night," he says. "But my bed might be a bit small for you."

You don't want to turn down the man's kindness, but you feel bad taking his only bed.

To take the offered bed, turn to page 40.

To insist Procrustes take the bed, turn to page 41

It has been a while since you've slept in a bed, so you accept the kind offer. You lie down, and your legs dangle over the edge.

"I'll see what I can do to fix it," your host says, and then he walks out of the room.

While waiting for him, you nod off. When you awake, you are tied to the bed. Then you see Procrustes carrying a large axe.

You scream as Procrustes raises the axe and cuts off one of your legs, right at the edge of the bed. Then he hacks off your other leg.

"There, now you fit perfectly," he says.

You pass out from the pain and bleed to death.

THE END

To follow another path, turn to page 12.

To learn more about Theseus, turn to page 99.

"I cannot take your only bed," you say, kindly. "It is too small for me anyway. It looks like it's better suited to you."

"No, no, I insist," Procrustes says. "It's too big for me."

There is something in the way he blocks your way out that worries you. Suddenly you don't trust him. Why is he so eager for you to sleep in his bed?

"I cannot. It's too small for me," you say.

"But I will make you fit," Procrustes says with a wicked grin. Then he pulls an axe from behind his back. "Just lie down!"

You were right not to trust him! He takes a vicious swing at you.

Turn the page.

You reach for your sword but realize that it is in Procrustes's smithy. You duck under his blow, and he flips over you, landing on the bed.

You notice that there are some straps on the bed. You use them to bind Procrustes by his hands and feet. You also notice that the ropes are attached to pulleys. You imagine that anyone who is too short for the bed would be stretched out by the weights attached at the ends of the ropes. And that is exactly what is happening to Procrustes. Once you tie him up, the ropes snap taut. He screams out in pain, and you make your escape. You continue on your quest, ignoring his pleas.

You reach Athens the next day. As you walk through the streets, people stop to stare at you. Stories of your brave deeds have spread throughout Greece. People call out your name as you walk by.

Turn the page.

The attention gets the notice of some city guards. They order you to come with them.

At first, you think they are taking you to the throne room to see your father. Instead, they lead you to a small, dark room. There, a woman waits.

"I am Medea," she says. "The king has heard of your brave deeds. But he wishes to know if they are exaggerated tales or if you are a true hero."

"I have overcome many dangers to reach Athens," you boast.

"Then you won't mind one more before you see your father," Medea says with a smile. "East of here, near the town of Marathon, a monstrous bull has been ravaging the area. Slay it, and prove you are truly a hero."

To accept the quest, go to page 45.

To insist upon seeing your father, turn to page 47.

"If I succeed, do I get to see the king?" you ask.

"You can dine with us," Medea replies slyly. "I will even make a toast in your honor."

"Then I will slay the Marathonian Bull," you say.

The hero Hercules had captured the Marathonian Bull and brought it to Greece years ago. Since then it has been wreaking havoc.

To find the bull, you follow the trail of wreckage and frightened people. You spot it on an open plain. It is nearly as tall as you and weighs much more.

When it sees you, it snorts and paws the ground. You raise your club as the bull rushes toward you. Once the bull is close, you bring the club down hard on its skull. The bull tumbles to the ground and lies still. With one swift swing you've defeated the mighty bull.

Turn the page.

You return to Athens greeted by cheers. The king holds a feast in your honor, as you sit by his side. Medea smiles and raises her glass of wine.

"To Theseus, our brave hero!" she shouts.

Everyone toasts, "To Theseus!"

You stand and raise your glass to your lips. But suddenly the king knocks it away.

"Don't!" he shouts. "Medea poisoned it. She told me you were a threat to my throne. But as you stood, I recognized your sword as my own."

You have survived many dangers to reach your father. He is overjoyed to finally meet you, and you are now heir to his throne.

THE END

To follow another path, turn to page 12.

To learn more about Theseus, turn to page 99.

You have overcome many dangers on your journey. In your opinion, you have earned the right to see your father.

"I have already proven myself," you proclaim. "Now take me to King Aegeus, for I am his son."

Medea's smile turns dark.

"That may be true," Medea says, "but my son, Medus, will be his heir. Guards!"

Two guards lower their spears while two others take your weapons.

"King Aegeus will never hear of you again."

Then the guards lead you down into the dungeon. You are locked away in a small, dark cell, never to escape.

THE END

To follow another path, turn to page 12.

To learn more about Theseus, turn to page 99.

CHAPTER 3

The Minotaur

You were shocked to learn that your father is the King of Athens. Determined to find him, you arrange for a boat to take you to Athens.

When you reach Athens, you head to the palace. The palace guards stop you. They don't care who you say you are.

"But I'm the king's son!" you shout. "See!"

You raise your father's sword. The guards take this as a threat. They raise their swords at you.

"Hold!" a voice commands from above. The king stands on a balcony above. "That is the sword I left in Troezen."

Turn the page.

"Father, it is I, Theseus!" you shout.

You are taken to your father, and he greets you with a hug. You tell him of your mother and of your journey to Athens. As you talk, you see an unmistakable sadness in his eyes.

"What is wrong, father?" you ask.

"You probably know that Athens lost the war with Crete," your father begins, and you nod. "But have you heard of the horrible price King Minos has exacted upon my kingdom?"

You shake your head.

"Every nine years, we send seven young men and seven young women to Crete. They are thrown into the Labyrinth, where the fierce Minotaur dwells. Their screams are heard as the beast hunts them down, one by one."

"You must stop sending them," you cry.

Your father bows his head. "Athens is not strong enough to survive another war with Crete," he whispers. "We have no other choice."

"But father, how can you — ?" you begin.

"And worst of all," your father interrupts, "it is time to send another group of tributes."

You jump to your feet and start pacing about the room. The thought of what happens to the young men and women who enter the Minotaur's lair horrifies you. Then an idea strikes you.

"I will go to Crete and stop this madness," you declare.

To go as one of the tributes, turn to page 52.

To go as a sailor, turn to page 54.

"I will go as one of the tributes," you decide.

"No!" your father says. "I'll never see you again. No one can escape the Minotaur's Labyrinth."

"It is the best way for me to sneak onto the island," you explain. "And if I kill the Minotaur there will be no more need to send the tributes."

You have made up your mind. You cannot let more people suffer. Your father doesn't agree, but he doesn't stop you.

When the ship is ready to leave with the tributes, your father meets you at the docks. He hands you a folded white cloth. You take it, unsure of what it is. Then he walks you to the ship. Unlike the other ships, it has black sails.

"The tribute ships use black sails," he says. "But on the return voyage, if your quest is successful, unfurl this white sail so I know you are safe."

"Of course," you agree.

"May the gods be with you," your father shouts as he waves good-bye.

The ship reaches Crete and docks in the capital city of Knossos. Before going ashore, you talk to the captain of the ship.

"Wait here for two days," you say. "If I do not return by then, assume I have failed."

You walk down the gangplank with the other tributes. Guards lead you to the city's center.

You walk past a man, about your father's age, reviewing the tributes. It is King Minos. Next to him stands a woman, about your age. She turns and meets your gaze.

To smile at her, turn to page 56.

To sneer at her in anger, turn to page 58.

The next day, you walk to the docks with your father. You recognize the ship sailing to Crete with its black sails of mourning. You and your father stop to watch the tributes walk up the gangplank.

"I will disguise myself as a sailor on the tributes' ship," you say. "Then I can sneak ashore."

You father hands you a white cloth.

"If you succeed," he says, "unfurl this white sail. Then I will know you have returned safely."

You agree and then say your good-byes. You board the ship. A stiff breeze fills the ship's black sails, and it shoots through the waves.

"Poseidon must favor you," the captain says.

You hope that is true, because once you reach Crete, you are not sure what to do. Somehow you must make it so that Athens never has to send tributes again.

Soon, you see the island of Crete on the horizon. The ship docks in Knossos, the island's capital city.

You leap ashore to help tie the ship to the docks. Then you ready the gangplank. The tributes march down it, one by one. You see the fear and desperation in their eyes. They are met by city guards, who line them up.

Then a man dressed in royal garb walks up to them. It is King Minos. He smiles and nods as he examines the tributes. Next to him stands a woman about your age. It is his daughter Ariadne.

To attack King Minos, turn to page 59.

To slay the Minotaur, turn to page 60.

The woman must be Ariadne, King Minos's daughter. You smile at her, and she blushes.

"Father, this must stop," she pleads. The king waves her off. She starts walking away, but not without glancing back at you.

You are held in a prison cell overnight. As you ponder how to defeat the Minotaur, you hear footsteps. It's Ariadne, sneaking in to see you.

"I've come to help you," she says. "What my father is doing is horrible and needs to stop."

"How can I defeat the Minotaur?" you ask.

"These items might help," she says. She holds out a sword, a spool of thread, a club, and a key. "You may take two. They are yours for a price."

To take the sword and spool of thread, turn to page 62.

To take the club and key to the Labyrinth door, turn to page 66.

You meet the woman's gaze with anger. She must be King Minos's daughter, Ariadne.

You are led to a prison cell to spend the night. The next day guards lead you to the Labyrinth with the other tributes and slam the iron door shut. You are plunged into darkness. The roar of the Minotaur echoes in the distance.

"We must stay together," you command.

But it does not matter what you do. You have no weapons, and you quickly get lost in the maze. One by one, the Minotaur kills your companions, until you are the only one left. By that time, you have gone days with no food and little sleep. When the Minotaur finally comes for you, you don't have the strength to put up much of a fight.

THE END

To follow another path, turn to page 12.

To learn more about Theseus, turn to page 99.

If you kill the king, perhaps it will end the need for the tributes. And this might be your best chance to do it. Once the king has counted the tributes, about half of the guards lead them away. He is poorly guarded and within striking distance. You draw your weapon and charge.

The guards near the king are slow to react. Just as you are about to strike, Ariadne screams. Her shout distracts you long enough for the guards to close in.

"Throw him in with the others!" King Minos commands, angrily.

You have failed in your quest. You become another of the Minotaur's victims.

THE END

To follow another path, turn to page 12.

To learn more about Theseus, turn to page 99.

The king is close, but there are too many guards nearby. Plus, his daughter is there. You don't want her to get hurt in a fight. Besides, killing the king probably won't save the tributes. They are sent into the Labyrinth as food for the Minotaur. That is who you need to kill.

The guards lead the tributes away. Then, instead of going back to the ship, you hide. At nightfall, you go in search of the Labyrinth.

You sneak through the city and toward the palace. It takes you all night to find the entrance to the Labyrinth. It is a large, iron door. But it is locked, and you have no way of getting in.

As you stand there, unsure of what to do, you hear quiet footsteps padding your way. You duck into the shadows. To your surprise, Princess Ariadne walks by.

She stops in front of the maze's door, and whispers, "Oh brother, I wish there were some other way to stop you and father."

"The Minotaur is your brother?" you say, as you step out of the shadows.

Ariadne steps back, surprised. "Half brother," she says, and then asks, "Aren't you one of the sailors from Athens?"

"I am," you admit. "I'm here to slay the Minotaur. To end the tributes."

"I could help with these," she says. She holds up a sword and a spool of thread. "They are yours for a price."

To agree and trust the princess, turn to page 62.

To distrust the princess, turn to page 68.

"What is your price?" you ask Ariadne.

"If you escape the Labyrinth, you must take me away with you," she says. "I can't stay on Crete, not after the things my father has done."

You agree, as you hold up the spool of thread. "But how will this help me?"

Ariadne tells you to tie one end of the string to the entrance of the maze. After slaying the Minotaur, you can follow the thread back to the door. Then, at nightfall, she will open the door to let you and the other tributes out of the maze.

Once she explains the plan, Ariadne wishes you good night and sneaks off.

The next morning, guards wake you. You have hidden the sword and spool of thread under your shirt, so they do not see them.

Along with the other tributes, you are led to a large iron door, the entrance to the Labyrinth. The guards shove you through, and then the door is slammed shut.

"Stay here," you tell the other tributes as you tie the thread to the entrance. "I have a plan."

You head into the maze. As you walk, you let out the thread behind you.

Shortly after you begin, you hear the hungry Minotaur bellow in the distance. You hope you can find him before he finds the other tributes.

Near the center of the maze, you find a large chamber. Its floor is covered with human bones.

"It must be the Minotaur's lair," you mutter.

In answer, the half-man, half-bull beast steps out of the shadows. He roars at you and charges.

Turn the page.

You duck his grasp and swing your sword. You cut the Minotaur across the thigh, and he stumbles. But he does not stop. He spins around and charges again, driving you back against a wall.

He lunges at you with his horns, but you roll out of the way. He crashes into a wall behind you, and that's when you see your opening. You drive your sword into his side, ending the monster's life.

After catching your breath, you follow the thread back to the Labyrinth's entrance and wait.

At nightfall Ariadne opens the door. You and the other tributes rush out of the maze. You follow Ariadne to the docks and quickly sail away on the ship that brought you to Crete.

Turn to page 69.

"What is your price?" you ask.

"Take me away with you," she says. "I can't stay here after what my father has done."

You take the club and the key from Ariadne.

"I will think about it," you say, as Ariadne leaves.

You now have a weapon to fight the Minotaur with and a key to open the Labyrinth's door.

In the morning, you hide the club under your shirt so the guards won't see it. They lead you and the rest of the tributes to the Labyrinth. The heavy iron door slams shut behind you. Some of the tributes cry in fear while others pound on the door.

"Hush," you say. "I'm going to kill the Minotaur."

You pull out your club from beneath your shirt.

"But how will we get out?" another tribute asks.

"With this," you say, holding the key.

You go in search of the Minotaur. You hear him before you see him. He snorts and rounds a corner coming face to face with you.

He charges. You duck and swing your club into his leg. He charges again. You roll away and strike him in the side. The Minotaur is bruised and bloody. You bring your club down on his skull, and he crumples to the ground, lifeless.

You have killed the beast! But you can't find your way back to the entrance. Turn after turn brings you to dead ends and more turns. At least the Minotaur is dead, so there will be no need for Athens to sacrifice any more young men and women. That thought brings you comfort while you starve to death in the Labyrinth.

THE END

To follow another path, turn to page 12.

To learn more about Theseus, turn to page 99.

"How dare you ask a price of me!" you shout. "Athens has paid a horrible price already!"

You bind Ariadne with thread from her spool. Then you discover that she has a key to open the Labyrinth door. You drag the princess into the maze with you. Then you hold up the key.

"If I slay the Minotaur," you say to Ariadne, "I will come back to let you out."

You head off into the Labyrinth's maze to battle the Minotaur. After several turns, he catches you off guard. The beast charges out of the shadows. You leap aside too slowly. You are slammed into a wall and crumble to the ground. The beast quickly ends your life.

THE END

To follow another path, turn to page 12.

To learn more about Theseus, turn to page 99.

You sail through the night, and the next day you reach the island of Naxos.

You decide to rest on the island for a few days. There, you and Ariadne realize that the Minotaur's death may not stop the conflict between Crete and Athens. But you have an idea. If you marry, surely your fathers will have to agree to peace.

That night, you go to bed feeling good. You have a plan that will solve all the problems Athens is facing. But as you sleep, a vision comes to you. In your dreams, you see Dionysus, god of wine and the harvest. He tells you that he wishes to marry Ariadne, and that you are to sneak away and leave her behind.

Suddenly you are awake. It is still the middle of the night.

To listen to the vision, turn to page 70

To marry Ariadne, turn to page 72

The gods have let you succeed in your quest, and you don't want to risk angering them now. You gather your ship's crew and the tributes and sneak away in the middle of the night.

You are saddened to leave Ariadne behind. In your grief, you forget to do as your father had asked. Your ship sails to Athens with the black sails of mourning.

When you arrive, you race to the palace. But you are stopped at the gate by wailing citizens. They tell you that your father had watched for your ship every day since you'd left. Upon seeing the black sails, he died out of grief, thinking you were dead. It is with a heavy heart that you are crowned the new ruler of Athens.

THE END

To follow another path, turn to page 12.

To learn more about Theseus, turn to page 99.

You have struggled so much to help your father and Athens that you are not going to give up on your plan. If you marry Ariadne, your father's kingdom will know peace for the first time in many years.

You go back to sleep with that thought in your mind. But you wake to screams.

"A leopard!" a servant shouts from the entrance to your tent.

You look around, but see nothing.

Then two guards rush into the tent. The servant points at you. "That beast must have eaten poor Theseus."

Suddenly you realize what has happened. Since you didn't follow Dionysus's wishes, he has cursed you, turning you into a wild animal.

The soldiers grab their spears and fling them at you. You dodge them and then dive past the guards and out of the tent. You escape, but not for long. More soldiers are outside your tent. They draw swords and quickly cut you down.

It is not until you are dead that you take on your human form again. Only then do the soldiers realize whom they have killed.

THE END

To follow another path, turn to page 12.

To learn more about Theseus, turn to page 99.

CHAPTER 4

Stuck in the Underworld

After retrieving the items left by your father, you say good-bye to your mother and arrange for passage to Athens by boat.

You reach your father's kingdom and head straight to the palace. You spot your father on a balcony. You draw your father's sword and raise it above your head to get his attention.

"Father, it is I, Theseus!" you shout.

Instantly, armed guards surround you.

"Hold!" the king commands. "It has been many years since I've seen that sword. Bring him to me."

When the guards bring you to him, he hugs you.

Turn the page.

"I'm so glad you've found me, my son," he says. "I'm sorry I never could return to Troezen," he explains. "But Athens was nearly destroyed in the war with Crete. It has taken me years to rebuild."

You are overwhelmed with joy to finally meet your father. But sadly, shortly after you meet him, he dies. You are crowned the new king of Athens.

During your time as ruler of the great city, you have several adventures. You journey with the mighty Hercules to battle the Amazons. You defend the city from invaders. You gain fame throughout Greece as a mighty hero.

Then, one day, someone steals a herd of your prized cattle. Whoever took them left a trail that is easy to follow. You find your missing herd grazing in a field. The culprit is waiting there with them. You can tell that he is no ordinary thief.

A sword hangs from the man's side. He walks with the confidence of a seasoned warrior.

"I am Pirithous of Thessaly," the man says. "And you are Theseus, I presume?"

"Yes," you reply. "Why did you steal my cattle?"

"I merely found a new field for them to graze in," Pirithous says with a smile. He rests one hand on his sword. "And I wanted to get your attention."

"Then I will take them back," you say, placing a hand on your sword.

"If you can win them back from me," Pirithous says with a wink.

He draws his weapon and charges you. You block him and strike back. He deflects your blow. This goes on for hours. The clanging of swords rings out until you are both exhausted.

Turn the page.

"I didn't believe it, but the tales about you are true," Pirithous says. "You are a mighty hero."

"Is that what this is all about?" you ask. "You're testing me?"

Pirithous gives you a playful wink and nods.

"I am a king myself," he says with a laugh. "I have no need for your cattle, but I could use a worthy ally such as yourself."

Pirithous holds out his hand for you to shake. Even though you are annoyed by his actions, he has also proven himself a mighty warrior. So you accept his friendship.

"Perhaps we can find a common foe to battle together," Pirithous says.

To battle Centaurs, go to page 79.

To battle the Calydonian Boar, turn to page 80.

Now that you and Pirithous have become friends, he invites you to his wedding. He is marrying Princess Hippodamia, from the city of Pisa.

A group of Centaurs are among the wedding guests. You are surprised to see these half-horse, half-man beasts. But Pirithous explains that Eurytion, their leader, is his half brother.

At the wedding reception, the Centaurs get wild and unruly. They stomp and shout.

"That's Centaurs for you," Pirithous laughs.

You aren't as dismissive of their rude behavior. You keep an eye on the Centaurs. At one point, you catch them harassing Hippodamia.

To stop the Centaurs, turn to page 82.

To tell Pirithous what is happening, turn to page 85.

You agree to go on a quest with your new ally.

"Have you heard of the Calydonian Boar?" Pirithous asks.

You shake your head.

"Well, King Oeneus forgot to offer the goddess Artemis fruit from the first harvest. So she sent a wild pig to ravage his lands," Pirithous says. "The king is calling for heroes to slay the beast."

You and Pirithous head to Calydon, the city ruled by Oeneus. There you meet other heroes who have come to battle the beast. There is Meleagros, the king's son. Atalanta is the fastest woman alive. Jason is famous for finding the Golden Fleece, a cloth made from the hair of a magical golden ram.

"Whoever slays the beast wins its hide as a reward," King Oeneus declares.

Then the hunt is on. Your hunting party combs the nearby countryside for the beast. You end up cornering it in a swampy meadow.

You and the other heroes circle around the massive boar. It has a thick, bristly hide, and it snorts and paws at the ground. Its tusks are nearly as long as your arm.

"How will we slay the beast?" Pirithous asks.

To attack with your spear, turn to page 86.
To let Atalanta attack with her bow, turn to page 87.

Even though the Centaurs are Pirithous's family, you don't like their behavior. They have stampeded through the wedding, and now they are harassing your friend's wife. You have had enough.

"Eurytion, leave her alone!" you shout.

While one of the Centaurs holds Hippodamia, Eurytion and the others turn to you. They are armed with clubs, and you are outnumbered.

"And who will make us?" Eurytion snickers.

"We will!" Pirithous shouts from behind you. Then he draws his sword. Behind him are more men, armed with spears and bows.

The Centaurs charge. Fighting with Pirithous, you slowly drive them back. The battle rages on. You find yourself face to face with Eurytion. He rears up, kicking out with his front legs.

Turn the page.

You dodge to the side and lash out with your sword, cutting him across the face. He reaches out to grab you, but you knock his hands aside. You strike with your sword, wounding him further.

The Centaurs realize they're fighting a losing battle, so they turn and flee.

"You are no longer welcome in Thessaly!" Pirithous shouts after them.

You are both bloodied and bruised, but you have won the day. However, many of Pirithous's kin died at the Centaurs' hands. Among them was Hippodamia.

"I'm sorry," you say to your grieving friend.

"You did all you could," he says. Your friendship is strong despite the day's tragedy.

Turn to page 89.

The Centaurs outnumber you, so instead of confronting them, you go find Pirithous. Together you rush back to where the Centaurs had been, but they are gone, and so is Hippodamia.

"Why didn't you stop them?" Pirithous shouts.

"There were too many," you say.

"You fool!" Pirithous cries. He angrily points his sword at you. "Leave. Leave now. I never want to see you in Thessaly again."

You do as Pirithous asks. That is the last time you ever see him. He wants nothing to do with you. And because of what happened at Pirithous's wedding, no other heroes want to join you on a quest. Your days of adventure are over.

THE END

To follow another path, turn to page 12.

To learn more about Theseus, turn to page 99.

The boar is huge, and you doubt an arrow would even be able to pierce its thick hide. So you lead the attack with your spear.

As the boar snorts and grunts, you prepare to strike. It squeals in anger. Then it charges you.

You brace yourself, holding your spear at the ready. But the mighty boar snaps your spear in half. You are now weaponless, and the beast is stampeding toward you. You can't get out of its way fast enough. As it knocks you over, one of its tusks gores your side.

Then the boar rushes off. The other heroes give chase. But Pirithous rushes to your aid.

It is too late. Your injuries are too severe. You die in your friend's arms.

THE END

To follow another path, turn to page 12.

To learn more about Theseus, turn to page 99.

You and the other heroes surround the beast. It snorts angrily and paws at the ground. The beast is enormous. You doubt any of you could survive its charge with just a spear.

"Let me weaken it first," Atalanta says.

She pulls an arrow from her quiver, fires, and pierces the animal's back.

The boar tries to shake the arrow loose, with no luck. With another arrow, Atalanta strikes the beast in the eye. It bellows in rage and charges.

The boar lunges one way, gouging one hero with its tusks. It leaps the other way, trampling another. You strike it in the back leg, and Pirithous wounds it in the shoulder. But it is the king's son, Meleagros, who deals the killing blow. He buries his spear deep into the animal's neck. It crashes to the ground.

Turn the page.

Back at the palace, King Oeneus awards the boar's hide to Meleagros. But Meleagros gives it to Atalanta.

"She drew first blood," he says.

Some of the other heroes grumble that a woman was recognized as the hero of the day. But you and Pirithous nod in approval, and no one will argue about Atalanta's right to have the hide if you two are on her side.

Go to the next page.

After your adventure with Pirithous, he comes to you with a strange proposal.

"As mighty heroes," he brags, "we should marry daughters of Zeus, ruler of the gods."

Zeus's daughters are some of the most powerful women and goddesses alive.

"Such as Helen of Sparta?" you ask. She is the most beautiful woman in the world.

"You should marry her, and I shall marry the goddess Persephone," your friend says.

Persephone is already married to the god Hades. But Pirithous is determined. You make a pact to go on a quest to capture the women.

Finding Helen in the Greek city of Sparta is easy. You capture her and bring her back to Athens. But Persephone lives in the Underworld.

Turn the page.

"How will we get in the Underworld?" you ask.

"Have you heard the story of Orpheus, the famed musician?" Pirithous asks.

You nod. After his wife died, he went to the Underworld to get her back. Pirithous claims to have found the secret entrance that he used.

Pirithous leads you across Greece to a strange rock formation. Between the rocks is a dark cave. You follow him into the darkness to the shores of the River Styx. There you see a tall, skeletal figure in a wooden ferryboat. It is Charon. You must pay him to take you across the River Styx. Pirithous drops a coin into the ferryman's palm and boards the boat. You do the same.

Without saying a word, Charon uses a long pole to move the boat across the river. The air is filled with eerie sounds of dead spirits calling out to you.

Turn the page.

You step off of the ferry. Next you must face Cerberus, the three-headed guard dog at the gates to the Underworld.

"How did Orpheus get by him?" you ask.

"He lulled him to sleep with a song," Pirithous says. "But I figure we can use these." Your friend holds up his sword and gestures to yours.

When you find the gates to the Underworld, Cerberus growls and snaps viciously at you. Before you attack, a deep voice shouts, "Stop!"

You turn to see a crack forming in the wall next to the gate. Through the opening, you see Hades on his throne. Beside him sits Persephone.

"What is it you want, mortals?" Hades asks.

"Merely to talk to Persephone," your friend says with his usual smile.

Turn the page.

The lord of the Underworld returns the smile. It seems as though he is agreeable to the idea.

"First let us dine together. I've heard tales of your bravery and wish to hear more," Hades says. He motions to a table set with a feast. "Sit down."

Next to the table is a stone bench.

"What do you think?" Pirithous asks, whispering in your ear.

To trust Hades, go to page 95.

To distrust Hades, turn to page 97.

"We have no choice but to trust him," you say to Pirithous. "We are in his domain, after all."

Your friend nods, and you both sit down on the bench. You start to eat, but as you grab a bunch of purple fruit, you forget what it is called. You turn to your friend to ask him, but now you've forgotten his name.

"Who are you?" you ask.

The man can only shrug his shoulders. He has forgotten how to speak.

As you sit there, in the Chair of Forgetfulness, all of your memories escape you. You forget why you are there, and who you are. You even forget how to stand. You are trapped.

This leaves the god Hades laughing. He has played another trick on some foolhardy heroes.

Turn the page.

Years later, all of your memories come rushing back as a muscular man pulls you from the bench.

"Hercules!" you shout. "What are you doing?"

"Rescuing you, apparently," he says.

"What of Pirithous?" you say. You now see that vines have wrapped around him and the bench.

"I can't free him," Hercules says. "I must be on my way. I am on a quest to capture Cerberus."

Hercules leaves, and you try to free Pirithous. But it is no use. You must leave him behind.

While your quest was not successful, at least you survived. You are one of the few mortals to ever escape the Underworld. The tale of your adventure will be one told throughout the ages.

THE END

To follow another path, turn to page 12.

To learn more about Theseus, turn to page 99.

"I don't trust him," you whisper to your friend.

"We are sorry to disturb you," you tell Hades. "Perhaps you could just allow Pirithous to talk to Persephone. Then we will be on our way."

"I do not have time for rude mortals," says Persephone. "Orpheus at least played me a song."

"Since you won't dine with us, I'll find another way to keep you here," Hades says. "Cerberus!"

The angry dog bursts into the chamber and leaps at you. Pirithous draws his sword, and you fight by his side as Cerberus charges. But you are no match for the vicious attack. You and your friend are now permanent residents of the Underworld. Your spirits drift to the Elysian Fields, where brave heroes go after their deaths.

THE END

To follow another path, turn to page 12.

To learn more about Theseus, turn to page 99.

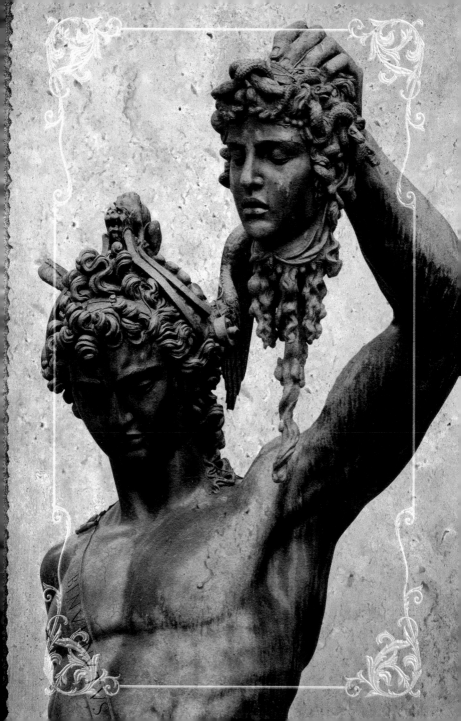

Chapter 5

Quests and Other Myths

The story of Theseus slaying the Minotaur is a popular quest myth. A quest myth is a story about a hero who goes on an adventure for a specific reason. The goal might be to find a treasure, as in the story of Jason and the Argonauts. Jason and his men seek out the Golden Fleece, a magical fabric made from the wool of a gold ram.

Often a quest myth involves a fearsome beast. The hero Perseus is known for defeating Medusa. Bellerophon fought the beastly, fire-breathing Chimera. Theseus battled giants, thieves, and animals to prove himself a hero, but he is most famous for slaying the Minotaur.

Turn the page.

Sometimes a hero might go on a quest to prove that he is truly heroic, as Hercules did. His most well-known quests are 12 nearly impossible tasks called "labors."

There are many exciting tales about heroes' brave deeds and the dangers they faced on their quests. But there are also myths about how the monsters they fought came to be. The Chimera had a lion's head, a goat's body, and a serpent's tail. It was said to be the offspring of Echidna and Typhon, two of the biggest and scariest monsters in Greek mythology. They were the parents of many horrific creatures. Medusa was cursed by the goddess Athena. Her hair turned into poisonous vipers and her skin became scaly. The curse made Medusa so hideous that anyone who met her gaze turned to stone out of fear.

There is also a myth about how the Minotaur and the Labyrinth came to be. The tale starts with Europa. She was the daughter of Agenor, a mythical ruler of the city of Tyre. This ancient city was part of Phoenicia, a kingdom along the eastern coast of the Mediterranean Sea. Zeus, ruler of the gods, fell in love with the Phoenician princess.

One day Europa was gathering wildflowers in a seaside meadow. A handsome white bull walked up to her. The animal was gentle, so she was not afraid. The bull bowed its head to Europa, as if asking her to go for a ride. Europa climbed up onto the bull. But the bull was really Zeus in disguise. Once Europa was on his back, he took off and ran across the sea. He carried Europa all the way to the island of Crete.

Turn the page.

Zeus and Europa had three children, among them Minos. Since he was a god, Zeus could not stay with Europa. He had to return home to Mount Olympus. Afterward, Europa married Prince Asterius of Crete.

After Asterius died, Minos and his siblings fought for control of Crete. Minos claimed that he had received the right to rule from Poseidon. He also said that the mighty sea god would give him whatever he prayed for. To prove this, he asked for a bull to sacrifice in Poseidon's honor.

Poseidon answered Minos's prayer. A giant bull rose from the depths of the ocean and presented itself to Minos. Because Crete was an island nation, the powerful sea god was an important deity. So receiving a gift from Poseidon sealed Minos's claim on the throne.

But Minos was greedy. He thought the bull was too magnificent to kill. He kept it and sacrificed another bull instead. Minos's broken promise angered Poseidon. As punishment, the sea god cursed Minos's wife, Queen Pasiphae. She fell in love with the bull, and they had a child, the half-man, half-bull Minotaur.

Minos was embarrassed by Pasiphae's beastly son. Worse than his looks, the hideous monster, also craved human flesh. The king asked the famous inventor Daedalus to build a prison for the Minotaur. Daedalus built the Labyrinth.

This maze had countless paths, twists, turns, and dead ends. It wound around endlessly, and no one but Daedalus knew the way out. The Minotaur lived within the Labyrinth until Theseus came and killed him.

Turn the page.

While mythic heroes may complete their quests and slay monsters, they often lead tragic lives. Jason lost his kingdom, and Perseus accidentally killed his grandfather. After being freed from the Underworld, Theseus returned to Athens. But much had changed during his years of imprisonment. His mother and Helen, his wife-to-be, had left the city. The people of Athens had forgotten about him, and another king now sat on his throne.

Theseus left Athens and eventually traveled to Scyros, a land ruled by King Lycomedes. While the people of Scyros welcomed Theseus as a hero, the king was jealous of his fame. Lycomedes worried that Theseus would take his throne. So one day, while the two were walking along a high cliff, Lycomedes pushed Theseus. He fell to his death in the sea below.

In fact, the lives of many characters in the story of Theseus and the Minotaur end tragically. Theseus and his father both die in awful fashion. Of course, the Minotaur is killed. King Minos mistreated Daedalus, so the inventor escaped from the island of Crete. Minos followed him to Sicily, and the ruler of Sicily had Minos killed in a boiling bath. Daedalus lived to a ripe old age, but his son, Icarus, died during their escape. Only Ariadne, who married Dionysus, avoided a tragic death. In some myths, she is given immortality by the gods.

While Theseus's story ends on a sad note, the people of ancient Greece revered him as a legendary protector of Athens. He was considered a national hero.

Turn the page.

The ancient Greek military leader Cimon claimed to have found the bones of the mythical hero. As the story goes, he brought them back to the city of Athens. Cimon then placed Theseus's bones in a shrine, giving him a place of great honor. Years later the city was under attack by Persian forces. According to the Greek historian Herodotus, soldiers defending the city saw Theseus's ghost. They believed he had once again come to the rescue of Athens, which spurred them on to victory.

GREEK GODS AND GODDESSES

Athena—goddess of wisdom and the protector of heroes. In many Greek myths, Athena provided heroes with help to succeed on their quests.

Hades—god of the Underworld and of wealth and riches. He is also a bit of a trickster and does not appreciate mortals invading his realm.

Persephone—goddess of the Underworld. Persephone was tricked by Hades into being his queen. As a compromise, she spends three months of the year in the Underworld with him and nine months on Mount Olympus with her mother, the goddess Demeter.

Poseidon—god of the sea and Zeus's brother. Poseidon was the patron god of Crete.

Zeus—god of the sky and ruler of the Greek gods. Zeus was the father of many of the most famous Greek heroes, such as Heracles and Perseus. His weapon was a thunderbolt.

OTHER PATHS TO EXPLORE

During his quests, Theseus had many adventures. You've just read some of the most well-known stories. These include his journey to Athens, the slaying of the Minotaur, and venturing into the Underworld. But what if Theseus had approached these challenges differently?

1. Instead of slaying the Minotaur, Theseus could have raised an army in Athens and then gone to war with Crete. Do you think he would have fared better than his father had years ago? Why or why not?

2. What if the Minotaur had escaped from the Labyrinth? What would happen then? How would Theseus catch and defeat him?

3. Pirithous and Theseus had an exciting and interesting friendship, though Pirithous was more of a daredevil. Theseus often felt pressured to do things he might otherwise not do. Do you think Pirithous was a good friend? Why or why not?

READ MORE

Ehrmann, Johanna. *Theseus and the Minotaur.* Jr. Graphic Myths: Greek Heroes. New York: PowerKids Press, 2014.

Hoena, Blake. *Everything Mythology.* National Geographic Kids Everything. Washington, D.C: National Geographic Children's Books, 2014.

Hunt, Jilly. *Greek Myths and Legends.* All About Myths. Chicago: Raintree, 2014.

INTERNET SITES

FactHound offers a safe, fun way to find Internet sites related to this book. All of the sites on FactHound have been researched by our staff.

Here's all you do:
Visit *www.facthound.com*
Type in this code: 9781515748212

GLOSSARY

crest (KREST)—to reach the highest point

labyrinth (LAB-uh-rihnth)—a complex maze

mortal (MOR-tuhl)—human, referring to a being who will eventually die

oracle (OR-uh-kuhl)—a person whom a god speaks through; Apollo used the Oracle of Delphi to give people guidance

patron (PAY-truhn)—a guardian or supporter

quest (KWEST)—a long journey to perform a task or find something

quiver (KWIV-ur)—a container for arrows

tribute (TRIH-byoot)—a payment made by one country to another as a sign of dependence

Underworld (UN-dur-wurld)—the land of the dead in myths

unfurl (un-FERL)—to spread, unfold, or shake out

BIBLIOGRAPHY

Apollodorus. *The Library (Bibliotheca)*. Theoi Classical E-Texts Library. http://www.theoi.com/Text/Apollodorus1.html

Barnett, Mary. *Gods and Myths of Ancient Greece*. New York: Modern Publishing Regency House, 1997.

Buxton, Richard. *The Complete World of Greek Mythology*. London: Thames & Hudson, Ltd., 2004.

Ovid. *Metamorphoses*. Theoi Classical E-Texts Library. http://www.theoi.com/Text/OvidMetamorphoses1.html

Plutarch. *Life of Theseus*. Theoi Classical E-Texts Library. http://www.theoi.com/Text/PlutarchTheseus.html

Stapleton, Michael. *The Illustrated Dictionary of Greek and Roman Mythology*. New York: Peter Bedrick Books, 1986.

Waterfield, Robin. *The Greek Myths: Stories of the Greek Gods and Heroes Vividly Retold*. New York: Metro Books, 2011.